BOOK 1

fun starter pieces for beginner pianists!

PiaNO

contents

Chester Music
part of The Music Sales Group
London/New York/Paris/Sydney/Copenhagen/Berlin/Madrid/Hong Kong/Tokyo

BeFoRe You PLay...

Are you sitting comfortably?

When you play, make sure your elbows are at the same level as your hands on the keyboard, so that your forearms are **parallel** to the floor.

You may be able to adjust the height of your stool or put a cushion on your chair so that you are sitting at the best level to play.

Always try to keep your arms and hands relaxed when playing.

Positioning your hands

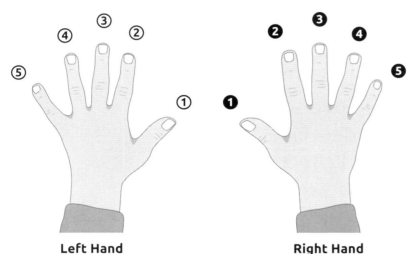

Left Hand   **Right Hand**

Finger numbers

The fingers of each hand are numbered from 1 to 5, starting with your thumb (finger 1) and numbering outwards to your little finger (finger 5).

Right hand position

Position your right hand with your thumb (finger 1) on **Middle C**.

Now put your other fingers down, one by one, on each of the next four white notes above (to the right of) **Middle C**: **D**, **E**, **F** and **G**.

Left hand position

Now position your left hand with your thumb on **Middle C** as well, sharing it with your right-hand thumb.

Then put your other left-hand fingers down, one by one, on each of the next four white notes below (to the left of) **Middle C**: **B**, **A**, **G** and **F**.

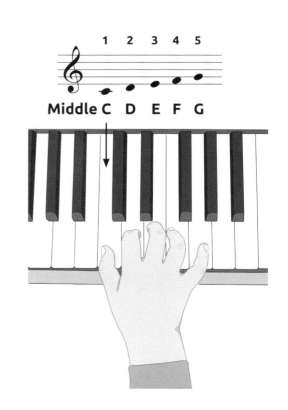

Middle C D E F G

Both hands

So, your hands should now be positioned with both thumbs on **Middle C**:

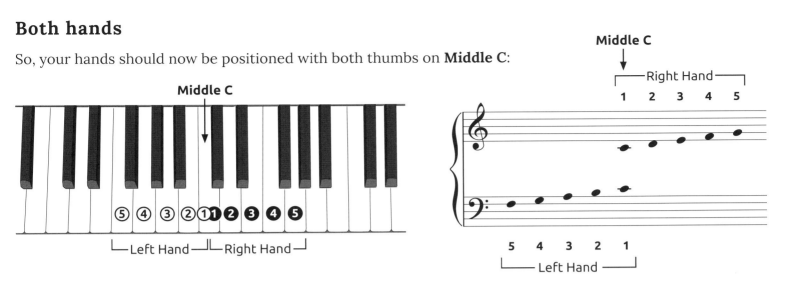

Position your hands correctly before you begin each song and you'll be off to a good start!

Note values and rests

This is a **crotchet** – it lasts *one count* and its rest is written like this: 𝄽

This is a **minim** – it lasts *two counts* and its rest is written like this: ▬

This is a **dotted minim** – it lasts *three counts* (𝅗𝅥 + 𝅘𝅥 = 𝅗𝅥.) and its rest is written like this: ▬·

This is a **semibreve** – it lasts *four counts* and its rest is written like this: ▬

The **semibreve rest** is also used to show a full bar's rest.

Preparing to play

Almost ready to begin now – but start by playing through these short warm-ups to get your brain working and fingers moving.

Jingle Bells

Words & Music by James Lord Pierpont

© Copyright 2016 Chester Music Limited. All Rights Reserved. International Copyright Secured.

Top tip

Watch out for the **dotted minims** in this song (in bars 6 and 10, for example) – they last for three counts each.

Count the full-bar rests (in bars 8, 24 and 32) to make sure you remain silent for four beats.

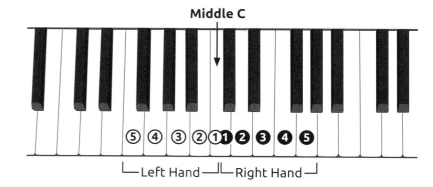

Briskly ♩ = 152

Accompaniment: Play the main part an octave higher than written when using this accompaniment.

5

Make You Feel My Love

Words & Music by Bob Dylan

© Copyright 1997 Special Rider Music, USA. All Rights Reserved. International Copyright Secured.

top tip

Count the four beats in each bar in your head as you play: "1, 2, 3, 4..."

When two notes are joined with a **tie** (between bars 3 and 4, for example), don't forget to hold the note for the full length of both notes.

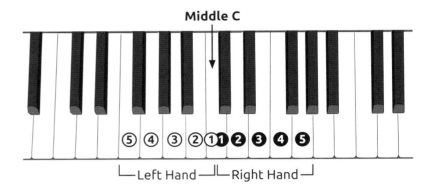

Middle C

Left Hand — Right Hand

Soulfully ♩ = 132

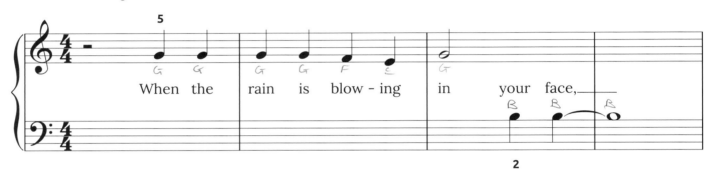

When the rain is blow – ing in your face,

and the whole world is on your case,

Accompaniment: Play the main part an octave higher than written when using this accompaniment.

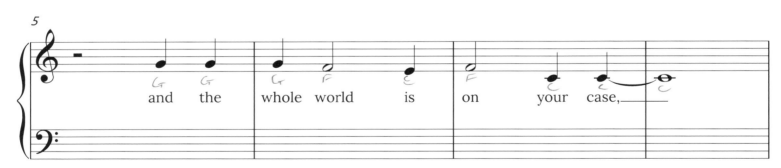

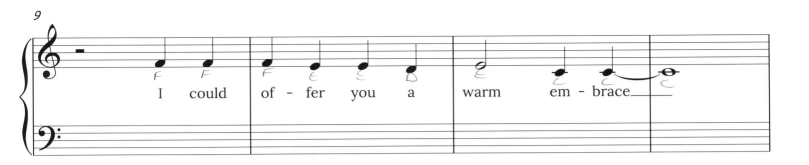

I could of - fer you a warm em - brace

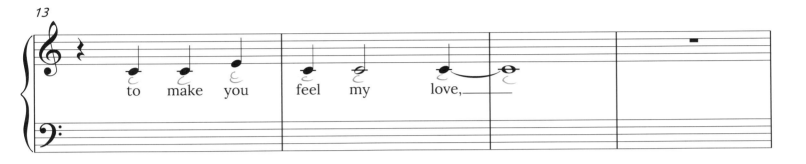

to make you feel my love,

to make you feel my love.

GHOST

Words & Music by Ryan Tedder, Noel Zancanella & Ella Henderson

© Copyright 2014 Write 2 Live Publishing/Songs Of Patriot Games/Blastronaut Publishing. Kobalt Music Publishing Limited/Sony/ATV Music Publishing. All Rights Reserved. International Copyright Secured.

top tip

Count the four beats in each bar in your head as you play, watching out for the rests.

In some bars you don't play anything on the first beat – can you spot where this happens?

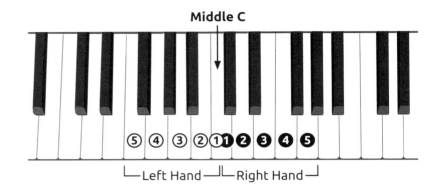

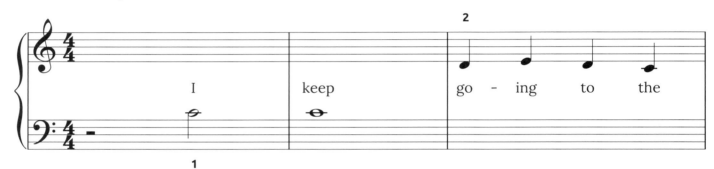

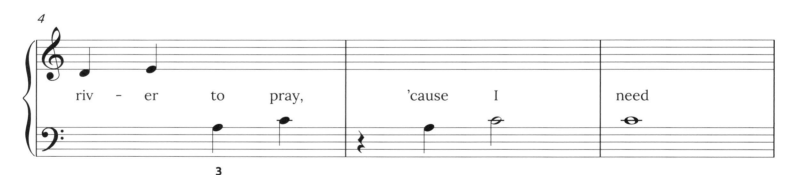

Accompaniment: Play the main part an octave higher than written when using this accompaniment.

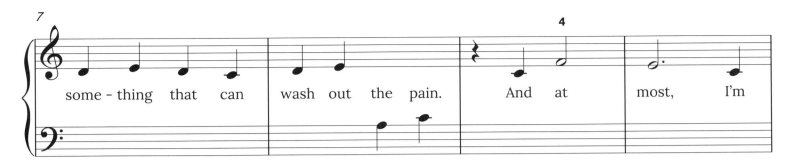

some-thing that can wash out the pain. And at most, I'm

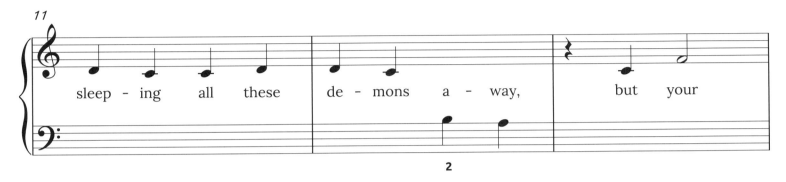

sleep - ing all these de - mons a - way, but your

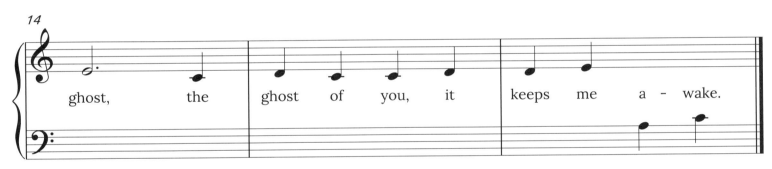

ghost, the ghost of you, it keeps me a - wake.

BReakING FRee (from *High School Musical*)

Words & Music by Jamie Houston

© Copyright 2006 Walt Disney Music Company, USA. All Rights Reserved. International Copyright Secured.

top tip

Before you play this song, clap the rhythm of the tune whilst counting aloud "1, 2, 3, 4…"

Watch out for the **ties** across bar lines – hold the note for the full length of both tied notes.

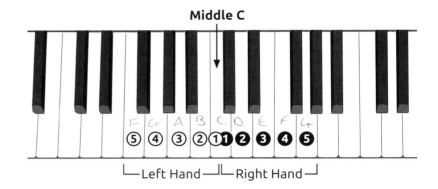

Energetically ♩ = 152

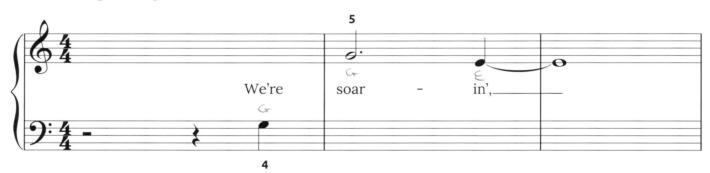

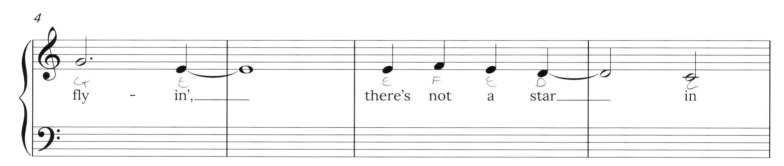

Accompaniment: Play the main part an octave higher than written when using this accompaniment.

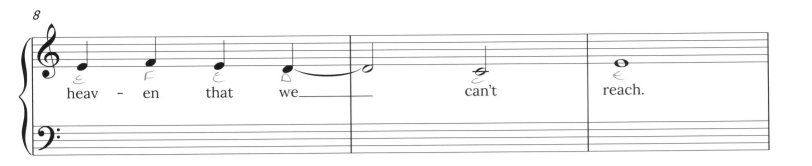

heav - en that we_____ can't reach.

If we're try - in',_____ yeah, we're break - in' free,

oh, we're break - in' free._____

3

BUDAPEST

Words & Music by George Ezra Barnett & Joel Laslett Pott

© Copyright 2013 BMG Rights Management (UK) Limited, a BMG Chrysalis Company/Chrysalis Music Limited, a BMG Chrysalis Company.
All Rights Reserved. International Copyright Secured.

top tip

Your left hand has more to play in this song.

Practise the left-hand part on its own at first, to make sure you are comfortable with the **bass clef** notes. Then work at playing it hands together.

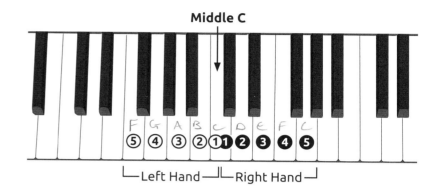

Lightly ♩ = 192

My house in Bu-da-pest, my, my hid-den

trea-sure chest,_____ gold-en grand pi-a-no,

Accompaniment: Play the main part an octave higher than written when using this accompaniment.

12

Some New Hand Positions...

Hand position for 'Halo' (page 16) and 'Barcarolle' (page 26)

Position your right hand as before, with your thumb on **Middle C**. Then position the thumb of your left hand on the note **B** just below **Middle C**.

Now put your other left-hand fingers down, one by one, on each of the next four white notes below (to the left of) **B**: **A**, **G**, **F** and **E**.

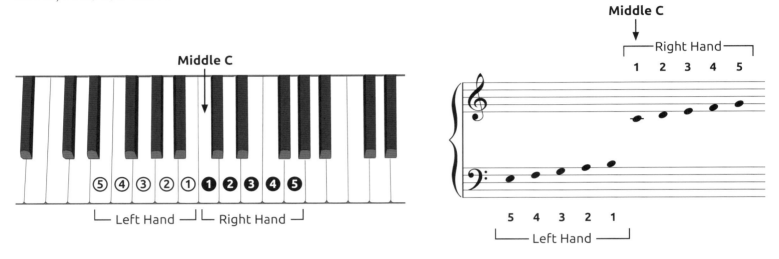

Try this warm-up before playing 'Halo' to get used to the new hand position.

Hand position for 'When The Saints Go Marching In' (page 18)

Position your right hand as before, with your thumb on **Middle C**.

Then position your left hand on the same notes (**C**, **D**, **E**, **F** and **G**) an octave lower.

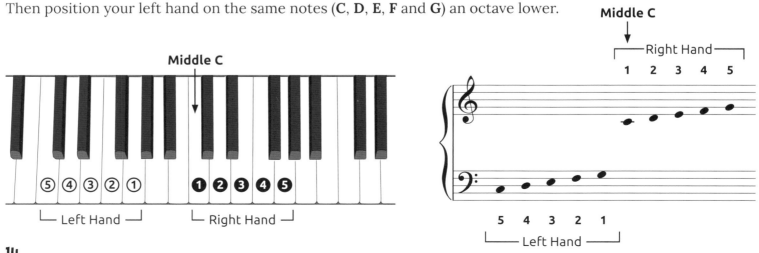

Try this warm-up before playing 'When The Saints Go Marching In' to get used to the new hand position.

Hand position for 'I Really Like You' (page 20)

Position the thumb of your right hand on the **D** one step above (to the right of) **Middle C**. Then put your other right-hand fingers down, one by one, on each of the next four white notes above **D**: **E**, **F**, **G** and **A**.

Now position your left-hand thumb on the same **D** as your right-hand thumb, and put your fingers down, one by one, on each of the next four white notes below (to the left of) **D**: **Middle C**, **B**, **A** and **G**.

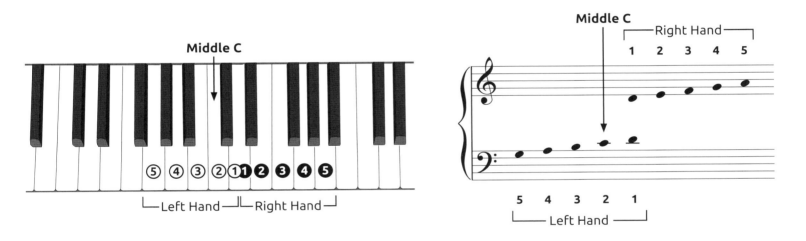

Try this warm-up before playing 'I Really Like You' to get used to the new hand position.

New note value and rest

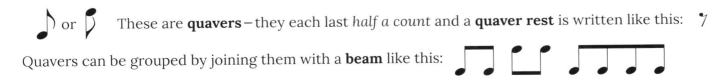 These are **quavers** – they each last *half a count* and a **quaver rest** is written like this: ♶

Quavers can be grouped by joining them with a **beam** like this:

Halo

Words & Music by Ryan Tedder, Beyoncé Knowles & Evan Bogart

© Copyright 2008 EMI April Music Inc./B-Day Publishing/Write 2 Live Publishing/Sony/ATV Songs LLC./Here's Lookin At You Kidd Music.
EMI Music Publishing Limited/Kobalt Music Publishing Limited/Sony/ATV Music Publishing. All Rights Reserved. International Copyright Secured.

top tip

Notice the different ways in which **quavers** can be grouped. Sometimes they are joined with a beam in four (bar 2) and sometimes in two (bar 4).

Sometimes they are not grouped, but written separately (bar 7).

Practise bars 7, 13 and 15 on their own before you play, to make sure you are confident with their rhythm.

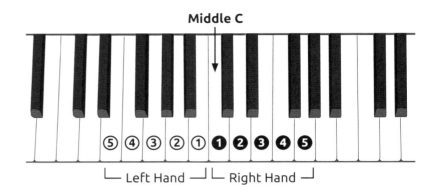

Middle C

Left Hand — Right Hand

Expressively ♩ = 132

p Ev - 'ry - where I'm look - ing now, I'm sur -

-round-ed by your___ em - brace.___ Ba - by, I can see your

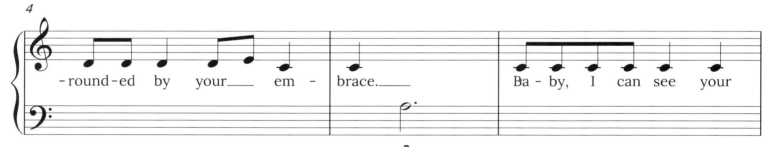

ha - lo;_____ you know you're my sa - ving grace. You're

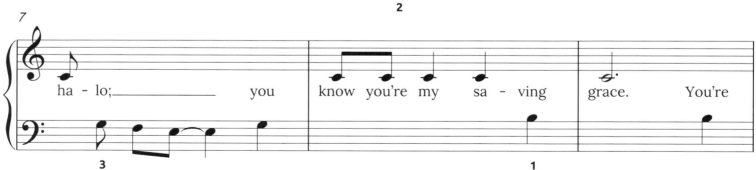

Accompaniment: Play the main part an octave higher than written when using this accompaniment.

10
ev - 'ry - thing I need and   more;___   it's   writ - ten all___ o - ver your

13
face.___   Ba - by, I can feel   your   ha - lo.___

16
f I can feel your   ha - lo,   ha - lo,   ha - lo,   I can see your

19
ha - lo,   ha - lo,   ha - lo,   I can feel your   ha - lo,   ha - lo,

22
ha - lo,   I can see your   ha - lo,   ha - lo,   ha - lo,   oo - oo.___

9

17

mf

17

WHeN the Saints Go MaRCHiNG iN

Traditional

© Copyright 2016 Chester Music Limited. All Rights Reserved. International Copyright Secured.

top tip

A **quaver rest** is written like this: 𝄾

In the bars that begin with a quaver rest, you start to play on the second quaver of the bar.

$\frac{2}{4}$ tells you there are two crotchet beats in each bar – count "1, 2..." in each bar in your head as you play.

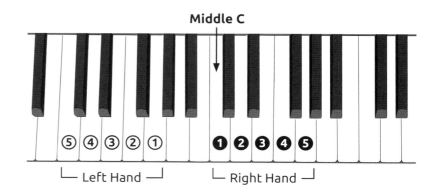

Chirpily ♩ = 72

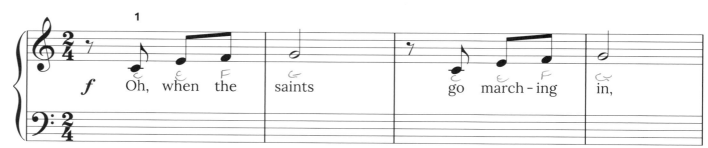

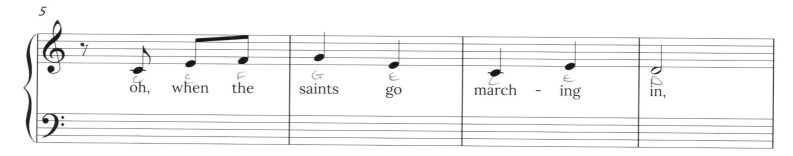

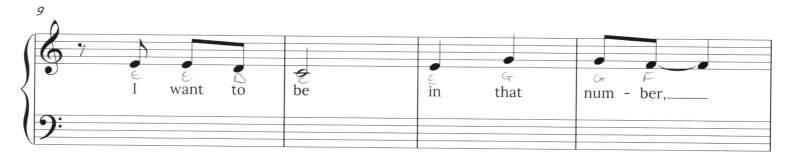

Accompaniment: Play the main part an octave higher than written when using this accompaniment.

i Really Like You

Words & Music by Peter Svensson, Carly Rae Jepsen & Jacob Hindlin

© Copyright 2015 Prescription Songs/Universal Music Corporation/P S Publishing/Jepsen Music Publishing/Virginia Beach Music.
Kobalt Music Publishing Limited/Universal/MCA Music. All Rights Reserved. International Copyright Secured.

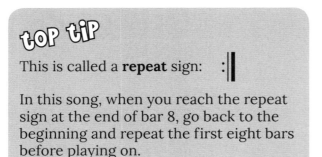

top tip

This is called a **repeat** sign:

In this song, when you reach the repeat sign at the end of bar 8, go back to the beginning and repeat the first eight bars before playing on.

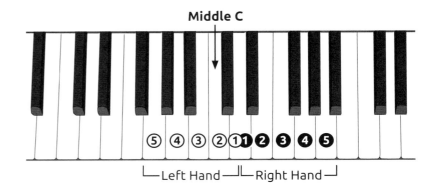

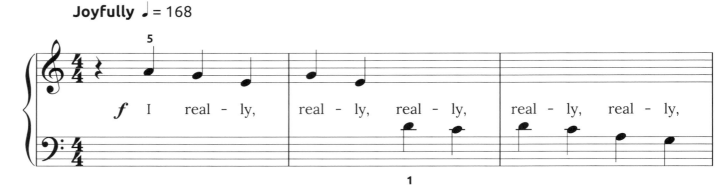

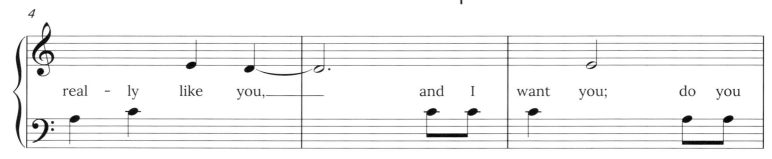

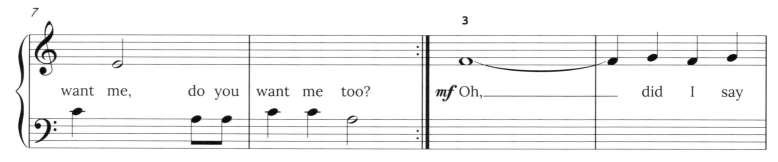

Accompaniment: Play the main part an octave higher than written when using this accompaniment.

Let it Go (from *Frozen*)

Words & Music by Kirsten Anderson-Lopez and Robert Lopez

© Copyright 2013 Wonderland Music Company Incorporated, USA. All Rights Reserved. International Copyright Secured.

top tip

This song uses the same hand position you used at the beginning of the book, with both your thumbs on **Middle C**.

There are many **ties** to watch out for – make sure you hold each one for the full length of both tied notes.

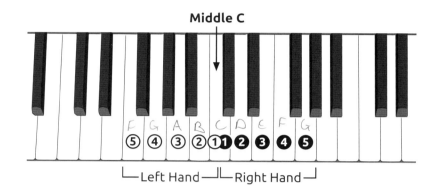

Powerfully ♩ = 144

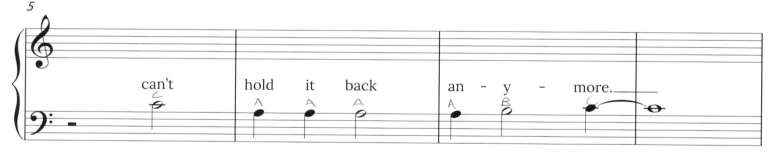

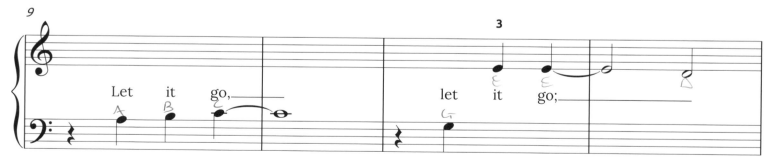

Accompaniment: Play the main part an octave higher than written when using this accompaniment.

22

HaNDs tOGetHeR...

In the next group of songs, you will be playing hands together!

Position your hands as you did for 'Halo'. Look at the diagram and description on page 14.

Now try the following warm-ups to help you practise playing hands together. Practise each hand separately at first, until you are confident – then put them together.

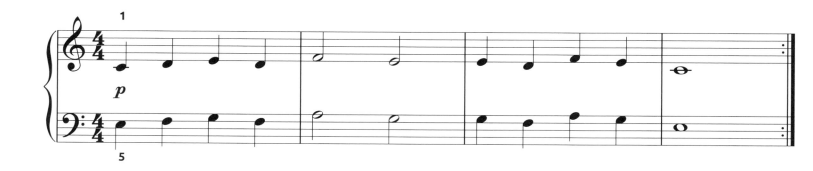

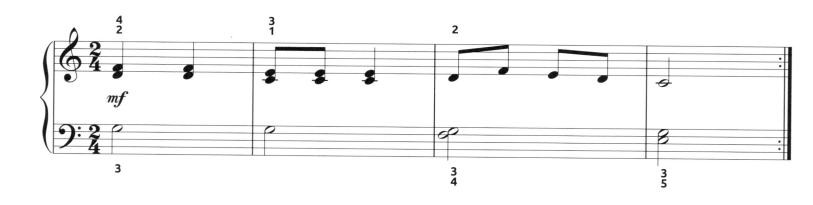

Flats   A **flat** sign ♭ lowers a note by one step (a **semitone**) to the very next key on the left.

New hand position for 'Shake It Off' (page 30)

Position the thumb of your right hand on the **D** one step above (to the right of) **Middle C**. Then put your other right-hand fingers down, one by one, on each of the next four white notes above **D**: **E**, **F**, **G** and **A**.

Now position your left-hand thumb on **Middle C** and put your fingers down, one by one, on each of the next four white notes below **Middle C**. Finally, move finger 2 of your left hand down a **semitone** to **B♭** (B flat).

So, from your thumb outwards, your left-hand fingers should be positioned on the notes: **Middle C**, **B♭**, **A**, **G** and **F**.

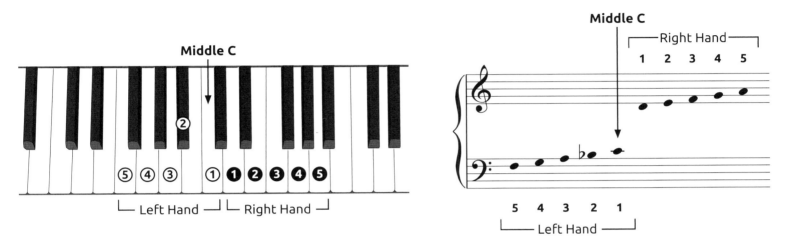

Try this warm-up before playing 'Shake It Off' to get used to the new hand position.

Barcarolle

Music by Jacques Offenbach

© Copyright 2016 Chester Music Limited. All Rights Reserved. International Copyright Secured.

top tip

This song uses the same hand position you used for *Halo* (page 16).

$\frac{3}{4}$ tells you there are three crotchet beats in each bar – count "1, 2, 3..." in each bar in your head as you play.

‖: At the start of bar 25 there is a **repeat** sign, which shows you where to repeat back from. When you reach the repeat at the end of bar 32, go back to bar 25 and repeat to the end.

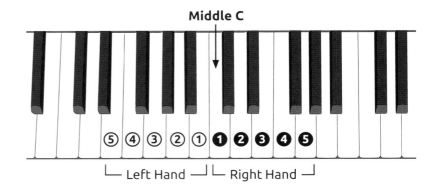

Middle C

⑤ ④ ③ ② ① ❶ ❷ ❸ ❹ ❺

└─ Left Hand ─┘└─ Right Hand ─┘

Sweetly ♩ = 104

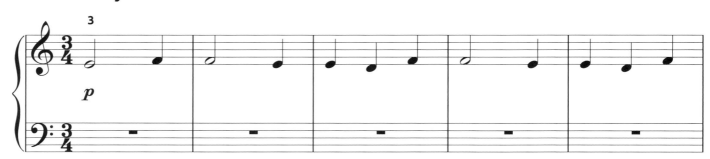

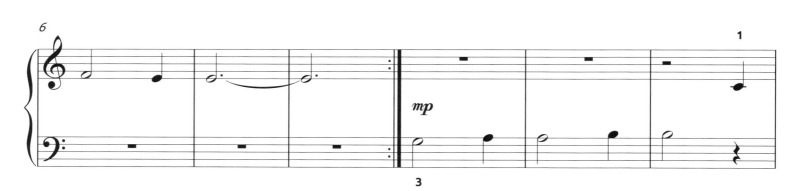

Accompaniment: Play the main part an octave higher than written when using this accompaniment.

everything is awesome! (from *The LEGO Movie*)

Words by Joshua Bartholomew, Lisa Harriton, Shawn Patterson, Akiva Schafer, Andrew Samberg & Jorma Taccone
Music by Shawn Patterson, Akiva Schafer, Andrew Samberg & Jorma Taccone

© Copyright 2014 Universal Music Corporation, USA/Warner-Olive Music LLC./Shebar Music/Boner Tek/Snuglar Entertainment/Drohnend Publishing.
Kobalt Music Publishing Limited/Universal/MCA Music Limited/Alfred Music Publishing. All Rights Reserved. International Copyright Secured.

top tip

This song uses the same hand position you used at the beginning of the book, with both thumbs on **Middle C**.

You will play with both hands at the same time from bar 10 to the end, so practise these bars hands separately to begin with, until you are ready to play hands together.

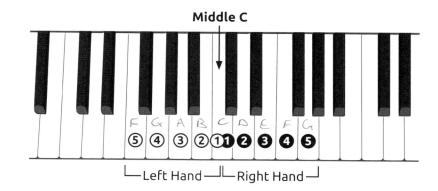

Spiritedly ♩ = 112

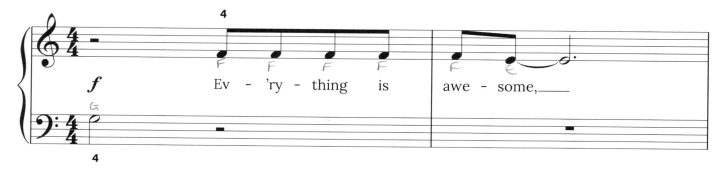

Ev - 'ry - thing is awe - some,___

ev - 'ry - thing is cool when you're part of a team;___ ev - 'ry - thing is

Accompaniment: Play the main part an octave higher than written when using this accompaniment.

28

29

SHaKe it OFF

Words & Music by Max Martin, Taylor Swift & Shellback

© Copyright 2014 Taylor Swift Music/Sony/ATV Tree Publishing/MXM Music AB. Sony/ATV Music Publishing/Kobalt Music Publishing Limited. All Rights Reserved. International Copyright Secured.

top tip

Look at the **key signature** at the beginning of each line – it tells you that all Bs should be played as B♭ (B flat). Make sure finger 2 of your left hand is positioned on B♭ before you play.

Don't forget to repeat the phrase between the **repeat** signs – bars 22–25.

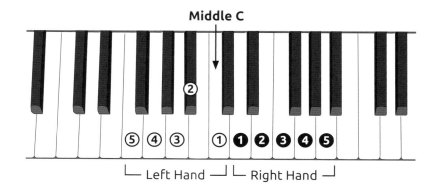

Middle C

Left Hand — Right Hand

Swiftly ♩ = 208

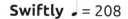

'Cause the play - ers gon - na play, play, play, play,

play,＿ and the ha - ters gon - na hate, hate, hate, hate,

hate.＿ Ba - by, I'm just gon - na shake, shake, shake, shake,

Accompaniment: Play the main part an octave higher than written when using this accompaniment.

30

123456789

Published by
Chester Music
part of The Music Sales Group
14-15 Berners Street,
London W1T 3LJ, UK.

Exclusive Distributors:
Music Sales Limited
Distribution Centre, Newmarket Road,
Bury St Edmunds, Suffolk IP33 3YB, UK.
Music Sales Corporation
180 Madison Avenue, 24th Floor,
New York NY 10016, USA.
Music Sales Pty Limited
Level 4, Lisgar House,
30-32 Carrington Street,
Sydney, NSW 2000 Australia.

Order No. CH84865
ISBN 978-1-78558-286-8

This book © Copyright 2016 Chester Music Limited,
a division of Music Sales Limited.

Unauthorised reproduction of any part of this
publication by any means including photocopying is an
infringement of copyright.

Edited by Toby Knowles.
This book devised and arranged by Christopher Hussey.

Printed in the EU.

Your Guarantee of Quality
As publishers, we strive to produce every book to the
highest commercial standards.
This book has been carefully designed to minimise awkward
page turns and to make playing from it a real pleasure.
Particular care has been given to specifying acid-free, neutral-sized paper
made from pulps which have not been elemental chlorine bleached.
This pulp is from farmed sustainable forests and was
produced with special regard for the environment.
Throughout, the printing and binding have been planned to
ensure a sturdy, attractive publication which should give years of enjoyment.
If your copy fails to meet our high standards,
please inform us and we will gladly replace it.

www.musicsales.com